INSIDE BATTLE MACHINES

TANKS
AND HEAVY
ARTILLERY

The crew of a Paladin, an American **self-propelled gun**, on manoeuvres in Kansas, USA

Thanks to the creative team:

Senior Editor: Alice Peebles
Picture Research: Nic Dean
Illustration: Martin Bustamante
Fact checking: Tom Jackson
Design: www.collaborate.agency

First published in Great Britain in 2017
by Hungry Tomato Ltd
PO Box 181
Edenbridge
Kent, TN8 9DP

A CIP catalogue record for this book is available from the British Library.

ISBN 978-1-910684-99-3

Printed and bound in China

Discover more at
www.hungrytomato.com

INSIDE BATTLE MACHINES
TANKS AND HEAVY ARTILLERY

The 12th-century trebuchet worked like a see-saw. A huge weight at one end dropped, making the arm rise to sling a stone ball high in the air.

by Chris Oxlade

HUNGRY TOMATO.

A British Challenger 2 main battle tank – one of the world's most advanced battle machines

Contents

[Highlighted words appear in the glossary]

TANKS AND ARTILLERY

Modern tanks, with their big guns and thick armour, are complex battle machines, crammed with the latest technology. They are devastating weapons in battle that punch holes in enemy defensive formations. Modern artillery is similarly high-tech. An artillery piece is a big gun. It delivers an **explosive shell** with great accuracy, often at a range of many kilometres. These amazing weapons are the result of a long history of development that began thousands of years ago.

British Mark 1

Length: 7.8 metres

Width: 4.2 metres

Weight: 28 tonnes

Engine: 16-litre petrol

Top speed: 6 kilometres per hour

Weapons: two 6-pound guns / three machine guns

Armour: 6- to 12-millimetre steel

Crew: 8

British Mark I tank
This was the first successful tank, introduced in 1916 to the battlefields of World War I. It had a gun in each side turret, machine guns and metal armour, but it was unreliable and easily damaged.

Old versus new

The two machines here show how the technology of tanks has changed over the last 100 years. Below left is a tank that fought in World War I (1914–18), the first war where tanks played an important part. Below right is a large modern tank, bristling with technology that makes it deadly in a fight.

M1A1 Abrams

Length: 7.9 metres	
Width: 3.7 metres	
Weight: 57 tonnes	
Engine: gas turbine	
Top speed: 72 kilometres per hour	
Weapons: 120-millimetre gun / three machine guns	
Armour: 600-millimetre **composite**	
Crew: 4	

M1A1 Abrams

This is a modern tank operated by the United States Army and other armies around the world. It features a powerful gun on a rotating turret that fires explosive shells, computerized gun aiming and armour made from advanced materials.

ANCIENT WEAPONS

Early artillery weapons were invented thousands of years ago. They were mechanical, having giant levers or springs to fire rocks, huge arrows and even dead animals at the enemy. There were also armoured machines on wheels. Many ancient weapons were designed for **siege** warfare: attackers tried to break down walls with heavy **projectiles** and battering rams, and fired projectiles over the walls to target the defenders.

An ancient arsenal

Here is a selection of ancient weapons for attacking troops and fortifications. These were all in use about 2,500 years ago. Some similar weapons were re-invented in medieval times, but often were not as good as the Roman versions.

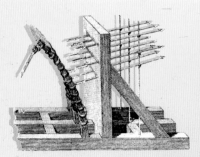

Arrow launcher This machine fired a hail of arrows in one go.

Mounted crossbow This was a giant crossbow on a stand that was aimed by hand.

Siege tower This tower was rolled up to defensive walls to allow attackers to storm battlements.

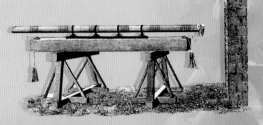

Suspended battering ram This type of battering ram was rocked backwards and forwards.

Sliding battering ram This battering ram was operated by pulling ropes, making it slide forwards and backwards.

Ballista This Roman machine was like a giant crossbow that fired spears or javelins more than 700 metres.

Onagar This machine used a tightly twisted rope as a spring to throw projectiles.

Siege warfare

During a siege, attackers often built tall, armoured towers on wheels, called siege towers or siege engines. They pushed the towers up against defensive walls, enabling soldiers to reach the battlements. This painting shows the siege engines at the siege of Constantinople (modern-day Instanbul) in 1453. By this time, early **cannon** were in use, too.

EARLY
CANNON

In late medieval times, a single innovation changed the world of weapons for good. That was the use of **gunpowder** in artillery, which would continue for hundreds of years. Gunpowder is a mixture of saltpetre, charcoal and sulphur, which burns very fast, creating a flash, a bang and lots of hot gas. Inventors realized that the gas could propel a stone or metal ball from a metal tube, making the first, simple cannon possible.

Chinese fire arrows

Gunpowder, or black powder, was probably invented in China in the 9th century CE, before its use spread to the rest of the world. The Chinese used it to launch rockets – known as fire arrows – at their enemies, and possibly in simple cannon, too.

Pot-de-fer

This 14th-century weapon's name means 'iron pot'. It was like an iron vase lying on its side, about a metre long, with a small hole leading into the centre. Gunpowder was poured into the pot, then an arrow-like projectile inserted. This had a leather-wrapped shaft for an airtight fit. Lighting the gunpowder through a touch hole shot the arrow away.

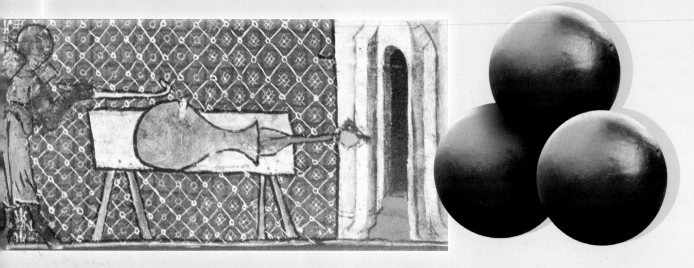

The Siege of Orleans

This 1428 painting of a famous French siege shows a typical late-medieval cannon. The cannon was made of lengths of **wrought iron** held together by iron hoops for strength. Later in the 15th century, cannon-makers began to **cast** bronze cannon, which were lighter and stronger than iron cannon. They remained the main type of cannon for around 400 years.

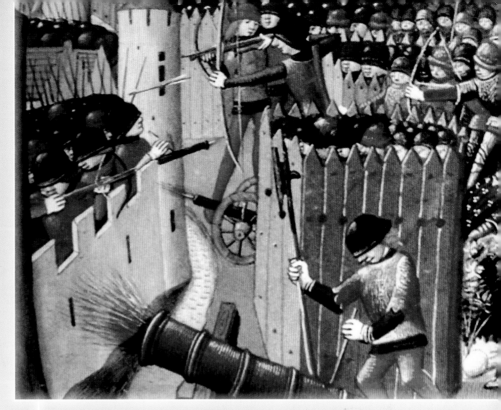

Bombard

Armies besieging castles and cities used massive cannon called bombards. They fired enormous stone balls that smashed defensive walls to bits. However, they were very hard to move around. This huge bronze bombard, now on display in the Russian capital, Moscow, is called the Tsar Cannon. It was cast in 1586, and was probably never fired.

IMPROVING ARTILLERY

The artillery of the early 19th century was not much different from the cannon of three centuries before. But from the mid-19th century, huge technical advances meant that artillery became more powerful, more destructive and more accurate. Explosive shells replaced solid **cannonballs**, powerful explosives replaced gunpowder, and artillery pieces became quicker to load.

Rodman 20-inch gun

Shown left is one of the largest guns of the American Civil War (1861–65). Thomas Rodman, a Union artillery expert, designed it. He invented a way of casting that made the barrel much stronger than ever before. The gun had a very large **bore** (internal diameter), and could fire a 0.3-tonne projectile more than seven kilometres.

Artillery in action

By the American Civil War, some guns had **rifling**: spiral grooves that made shells spin as they hurtled along the barrel. It made them fly much straighter than from older 'smoothbores'. These guns were **muzzle loaders**: the **propellant** charge was pushed down the barrel first, then the ball or shell.

Siege mortar

In a **mortar**, the barrel is quite short compared to its diameter. Its job is to throw a very heavy explosive charge high into the air, so that the charge lands almost vertically. This mortar, nicknamed The Dictator, saw action at the Siege of Petersburg during the American Civil War, where it destroyed Confederate gun emplacements.

The Dictator

Barrel length:	135 centimetres
Bore diameter:	33 centimetres
Weight:	7.8 tonnes
Projectile:	100-kilogram mortar shell
Range:	4 kilometres
Date:	1862

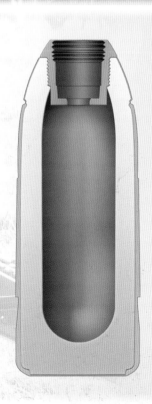

The shell

A shell is a hollow projectile, filled with explosive. Simple gunpowder-filled shells were in use by the 16th century. In 1784, British artillery officer Henry Shrapnel invented a shell filled with bullets and an explosive charge. The charge blew the shell apart in mid-air, releasing a deadly shower of bullets. All modern shells are cylindrical in shape, with a pointed end. The shell shown here was developed in the mid-19th century.

THE FIRST
ARMOURED VEHICLES

The idea of an armoured battle vehicle is thousands of years old. In ancient times, warriors went into battle on chariots; and the siege tower could be thought of as a simple armoured vehicle. Proper armoured vehicles became possible with the development of mechanical power, such as the steam engine and the internal combustion engine in the 19th century.

Chariots

Warriors first charged into battle on chariots more than 4,000 years ago. These fast, two-wheeled carts had a shield at the front, and the warrior was armed with a bow and arrow, spears and swords. This mosaic shows Alexander the Great fighting from a chariot.

Leonardo da Vinci's tank

A sketch drawn in about 1485 by the famous Italian artist and engineer Leonardo da Vinci shows a mobile armoured vehicle armed with small guns. This model was made from studying the sketch – the vehicle was never made. The sketch shows that the machine would have been moved by hand cranks inside.

Model-T fighting car

Early mechanized gun carriers, such as this 1913 British Model-T MG, were cars (here a Model-T Ford) with machine guns added to them. Hundreds of these were used as armed patrol cars in desert warfare in World War I, looking out for the enemy and ready to attack.

Simms Motor War Car

Length: 8.5 metres

Width: 2.4 metres

Armour: 6-millimetre steel

Weapons: two Maxim machine guns

Engine: 3.3-litre petrol

Crew: 4

Simms Motor War Car

This extraordinary British machine was the first fully armoured fighting vehicle, and was completed in 1902. The designer and builder was Frederick Simms. Simms started with a chassis from a large motor car with its petrol engine, and added a body of 6-millimetre armour plate, with pointed ends for ramming. The machine was never used in battle, however.

BIG GUNS

Artillery played an enormous part in World War I. Armies dug hundreds of kilometres of defensive trenches and attacked each other with huge artillery barrages, which often lasted for many hours. Most of the time the enemy was far away and out of sight, but gunners used information from spotters, and some maths, to work out which way to aim their guns.

World War I artillery

These Belgian gunners set up their field artillery on the Western Front during World War I. The gun has a metal shield to protect the crew from gunfire and **shrapnel**. The positions of enemy guns were found by observing their sounds and flashes from different positions on the front line.

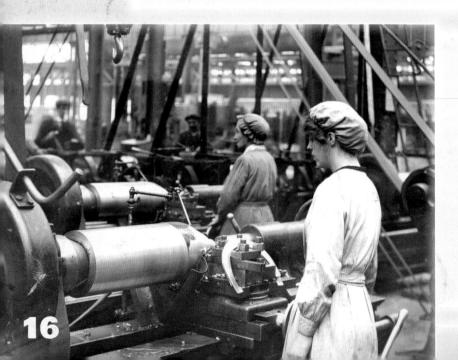

Ammunition supplies

The big guns of World War I needed a constant supply of shells. These were made in giant ammunition factories such as this one in Britain. As well as high-explosive shells, there were shells for producing smoke across the battlefield, and incendiary shells that spread fire.

Monster guns

During World War II (1939–45), the Germans built enormous guns for launching massive high-explosive shells at targets dozens of kilometres way. The gun pictured, named Dora, was the biggest of the war. It fired shells 80 centimetres in diameter and weighed nearly 5 tonnes! They could penetrate seven metres of concrete, or a metre of solid steel. Dora was mounted on railway bogies that moved along two parallel railway tracks.

Big gun in action

Dora was ready for action in the Soviet Union (now Russia), but was never used. Another similar gun, called Heavy Gustav, was used when Germany invaded the Soviet Union in 1941–42, to attack the city of Sevastopol in the Crimea.

Railway Gun 'Dora'

Length: 47 metres

Width: 7 metres

Barrel length: 33 metres

Bore diameter: 80 centimetres

Weight: 1,350 tonnes

Range (4.8-tonne high-explosive shell): 39 kilometres

THE FIRST TANKS

Before World War I began, the military authorities in most countries didn't think tanks would be useful on the battlefield, as they were used to fighting with foot soldiers and horses. But World War I became a war from trenches, with armies dug in, facing each other across shell-hole-covered battlefields. Generals soon realized that an armoured vehicle with weapons, which could move across the rough, muddy ground, would be useful for attacking enemy positions.

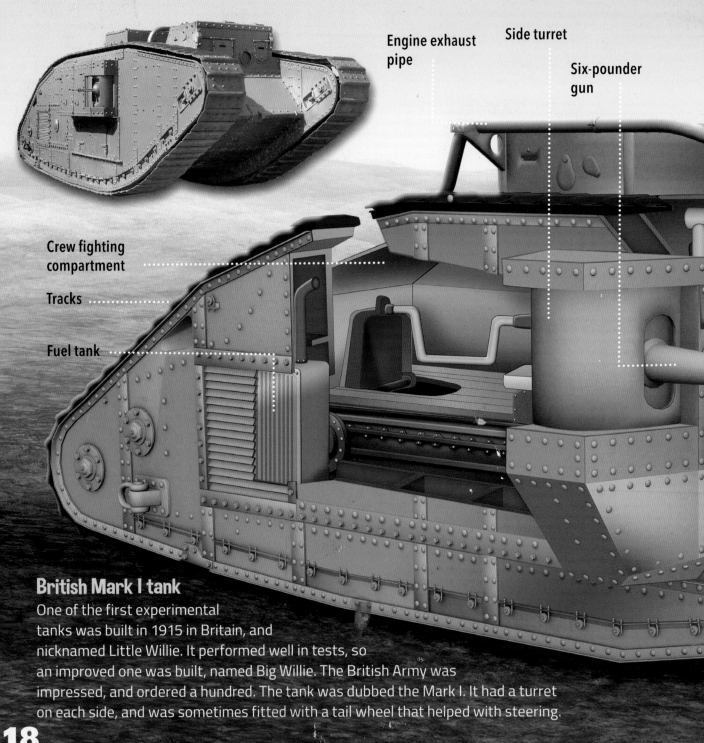

Engine exhaust pipe

Side turret

Six-pounder gun

Crew fighting compartment

Tracks

Fuel tank

British Mark I tank

One of the first experimental
tanks was built in 1915 in Britain, and
nicknamed Little Willie. It performed well in tests, so
an improved one was built, named Big Willie. The British Army was
impressed, and ordered a hundred. The tank was dubbed the Mark I. It had a turret
on each side, and was sometimes fitted with a tail wheel that helped with steering.

The Battle of Cambrai

The Mark I tank had faults. It was slow, the tracks often broke and the engine often stalled. In 1917, however, 474 much-improved Mark VI tanks took part in the Battle of Cambrai. They broke through the German lines. The battle showed that tanks had come of age.

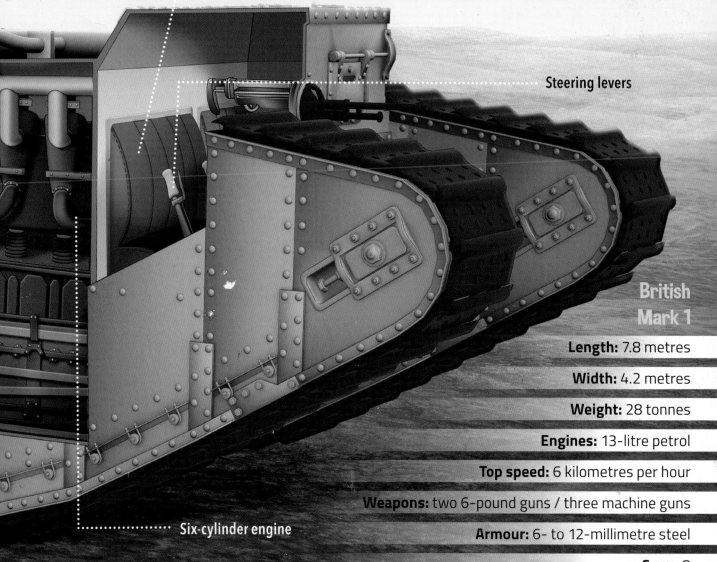

Driver's cab

Steering levers

Six-cylinder engine

British Mark 1

Length:	7.8 metres
Width:	4.2 metres
Weight:	28 tonnes
Engines:	13-litre petrol
Top speed:	6 kilometres per hour
Weapons:	two 6-pound guns / three machine guns
Armour:	6- to 12-millimetre steel
Crew:	8

TANKS OF WORLD WAR II

After World War I, tanks became bigger, faster and better armed and armoured. World War II began with devastating attacks by huge formations of German tanks – the **panzer** divisions. Germany and the Soviet Union built even larger and more powerful tanks as war continued.

M4 Sherman

The M4 Sherman was the main Allied tank of World War II. The Sherman was built for speed and mobility rather than firepower and armour. In a one-on-one fight it was no match for German Tiger (below) and **Panther** tanks, but it was successful fighting in packs.

The German Tiger

The German Panzer VI tank, the 'Tiger', was huge and formidable. It weighed 54 tonnes and had an 88-millimetre gun designed to knock out smaller Russian tanks. In 1944, the Germans introduced the Tiger II, a true monster, weighing 69 tonnes.

The Russian T-34

The T-34 was the main Russian tank of World War II. At 28 tonnes, it was a medium rather than a heavy tank. But its 76-millimetre gun could destroy all but the biggest German tanks. Also, its thick armour sloped, making shells bounce off.

Panzer VI 'Tiger' (below left)

Length:	6.3 metres
Width:	3.6 metres
Weight:	54 tonnes
Engine:	Maybach V-12
Top speed:	45 kilometres per hour
Weapons:	88-millimetre gun / 2 machine guns
Armour:	25- to 120-millimetre steel
Crew:	5

Eastern front battles

Russian T-34s (above and right) and German Tigers were some of the tanks that fought on the Eastern Front, in 1942–45. In 1943, the Germans, pushed back by the Russians, made a stand near the Russian city of Kursk. Around 3,000 Germans and around 6,000 Russian tanks were involved in the Battle of Kursk. It was the largest tank battle in history, and a victory for the Russians.

MODERN ARTILLERY

Even though tanks carry powerful guns, armies still use artillery pieces to attack enemy positions. All modern artillery is **field artillery** – it can be moved to where it's needed. There are two types: towed artillery, which is towed from place to place; and self-propelled artillery, where the artillery piece is mounted on a vehicle. Artillery can also be moved by helicopter.

Rocket launchers

Rockets are self-propelled projectiles with rocket engines and an explosive charge. Rocket launchers are often thought of as artillery, although the rockets are self-propelled rather than fired by a gun. This is a Russian Buratino multiple rocket launcher (MRL).

Modern shells

Shells are cylindrical with a pointed end. The main type is the high-explosive (HE) shell. This is a metal canister containing an explosive charge and a fuse. The fuse sets off the charge when the shell arrives at its target. Other types include the armour-piercing shell, the illuminating shell, which lights up a battlefield, and the smoke shell.

Self-propelled artillery

A self-propelled (SP) artillery piece is a cross between a tank and a gun. Here, inside an American M109 Paladin, the 155-millimetre gun is ready to fire. The crew is protected from small-arms fire and explosions outside by thin armour.

M198 Howitzer

Barrel length:	6.1 metres
Length:	11 metres
Weight:	7.2 tonnes
Bore diameter:	155 millimetres
Weight:	7.2 tonnes
Crew:	9
Maximum range:	22 kilometres

Field howitzer

A modern field gun is towed into position by a support truck, which carries the crew, ammunition and other equipment. In position, the gun's legs are folded out to stabilize it. The gun is aimed by swivelling it from side to side, and angling the barrel to adjust the range.

MODERN TANKS

Modern tanks still look remarkably similar to the tanks that fought in World War II – they have an armoured body, two tracks, a revolving turret and a big gun. However, modern tanks have better speed and handling, and stronger armour, making them safer for their crews. They also have computerized targeting and aiming systems, so their guns are very accurate, even when they are moving on rough ground.

Firing the gun

On top of the tank is a digital sighting system to identify targets such as other tanks. The crew selects one of the targets, and the angles of the turret and the gun are automatically adjusted so the shell will hit the target. Tanks fire armour-piercing shells to knock out enemy tanks. These pierce through armour before exploding.

Challenger 2

The British Challenger 2 tank has a 120-millimetre gun controlled by a laser rangefinder and a digital fire computer. The Challenger 2 has some of the toughest armour of any modern tank. The hull and turret are protected by Chobham armour, made from a composite material comprising ceramics, metals and plastics.

Crew protection

The Leopard 2A6 (right) is the German army's main battle tank. As in other modern tanks, the crew is protected inside an airtight compartment. In a nuclear, biological or chemical (NBC) attack, air is filtered as it goes in. There is also a system for putting out fires instantly.

Challenger 2

Length: 8.3 metres

Width: 3.5 metres

Weight: 62.5 tonnes

Engines: diesel V-12

Top speed: 59 kilometres per hour

Weapons: 120-millimetre gun/ chain gun/ machine gun

Armour: composite

Crew: 4

ABRAMS BATTLE TANK

The M1 Abrams is one of the most technically advanced tanks in the world. It's a heavy, well-armed and well-armoured machine, and is the main tank of the US Army and US Marine Corps. More than 10,000 of these tanks have been built. There are three versions: the original M1, the M1A1 and the M1A2, each one being an improvement on the last.

M1A1 Abrams

Length: 7.9 metres

Width: 3.7 metres

Weight: 57 tonnes

Engine: gas turbine

Top Speed: 72 kilometres per hour

Weapons: 120-millimetre gun/ three machine guns

Armour: composite

Crew: 4

Remote weapons system (gun fired from inside tank)

The 120-millimetre gun is controlled by a digital fire control system, which improves accuracy by taking into account wind speed, air pressure and the shape of the shell being fired.

Driver's controls

Driver's position

Machine gun

Gas turbine engine

Wheels that drive tracks

The ammunition store separates from the turret in case of a direct hit, protecting the crew from explosions.

The crew is protected in their compartment from nuclear, biological and chemical attack.

Tracks made from linked metal sections

Composite armour is made of layers of different materials, so it is tougher than solid steel.

TIMELINE

12th century
The trebuchet, similar to the catapult, is developed in Europe

14th century
Simple weapons using gunpowder, such as the pot-de-fer, are invented

1485
Leonardo da Vinci sketches a man-powered armoured fighting vehicle

1586
The enormous bombard called the Tsar cannon is cast

19th century
Cylinder-shaped explosive shells that explode on impact are developed

1861-65
Guns with rifled barrels are used widely during the American Civil War

1914-18
Artillery is used on a massive scale to attack enemy trenches during World War I

1917
British Mark IV tanks break through German lines at the Battle of Cambrai

9th century CE
Gunpowder is invented in China

c. 500 BCE
Armies of Greece and Rome are using a range of weapons such as battering rams and giant crossbows

1428
Simple cannon are used at the Siege of Orleans in France

1784
Henry Shrapnel invents a shell that releases bullets, now known as the Shrapnel shell

1453
Wrought-iron cannon help in the siege of Constantinople (modern-day Instanbul)

1940
The first Russian T-34 tank is built

1939-45
Powerful tanks are used for high-speed attacks on the enemy during World War II

1915
The first experimental tanks are built in Britain, and are first used in battle the same year

c. 2000 BCE
Warriors are going into battle in horse-drawn chariots

1902
In England, Frederick Simms builds the Simms Motor War Car, an early armoured car

FACT FILE

1942

The first German Tiger tank goes into action

1998

The first British Challenger 2 tank goes into service

1979

The M198 Howitzer goes into service

1980

The first American M1 Abrams tank goes into service

- The German Tiger II tank was so heavy that bridges would collapse under its weight. So Tiger IIs had watertight hatches and a snorkel so they could drive through rivers up to 4 metres deep.

- World War II began with sweeping attacks by hundreds of German tanks, known as the panzer divisions. Nothing could stop them.

- Today the word 'shrapnel' means a piece of metal from a shell. The word comes from Henry Shrapnel, who invented an exploding shell.

- British guns fired nearly two million shells at the German line in a few days at the start of the Battle of the Somme in 1916.

- The largest tank ever to go into mass production was the French Char 2C, which was 10.2 metres long and weighed 69 tonnes. It was used between 1921 and 1940.

- The heaviest tank ever built was the Panzerkampfwagen VIII Maus (the Mouse), weighing 188 tonnes. Only one Mouse was completed.

- During World War I, the British built a giant explosives factory in Scotland. The explosives were dangerous to handle, because they could easily explode, and the sloppy mixture of chemicals used to make them was known as 'Devil's Porridge'.

GLOSSARY

A siege tower, often used to storm castle walls under siege

Bore
The inner diameter of a gun's barrel

Breech loader
A gun in which the propellant and projectile are loaded into the rear of the gun through a door called a breech

Cannon
An artillery piece that uses gunpowder or other explosive material to launch a projectile

Cannonball
A solid ball of iron or stone fired from a cannon

Cast, casting
A process of forming a material into shape by melting it and pouring it into a mould

Composite
A material made from two or more other materials combined together

Explosive
A substance that burns so fast it creates a shock wave in the air that destroys everything around it

Field gun
A gun that moves around the battlefield

Gas turbine engine
An engine in which gas from burning fuel passes through a fan-like turbine, making the turbine spin

Gunpowder
A grey powder that burns fast and explodes, producing heat and gas

Howitzer
An artillery piece that fires a heavy projectile high in the air so that it falls downwards towards its target

Mortar
A short-range artillery piece

Muzzle loader
A gun in which the propellant and projectile are loaded down the gun's muzzle (open end)

18th-century cannonball

A muzzle-loading artillery piece from the American Civil War

Panther
A German medium-sized tank of World War II

Panzer
The German word for a tank

Projectile
Any object fired through the air

Propellant
An explosive charge that pushes a cannonball or shell from a gun

Range
The distance from a gun to its target, or the maximum distance that the gun can fire

Rifling
Grooves on the inside of a gun's barrel that make a shell spin as it's fired

Self-propelled gun
A vehicle with a large gun but no armour

Shell
A metal cylinder with a pointed end that is fired from a gun and which explodes on impact

Shrapnel
A piece of metal shell case released when a shell explodes

Siege
A battle in which a defending army locks itself inside the walls of a city or castle, and an attacking army tries to break in

Wrought iron
A pure form of iron, easy to shape but not stiff

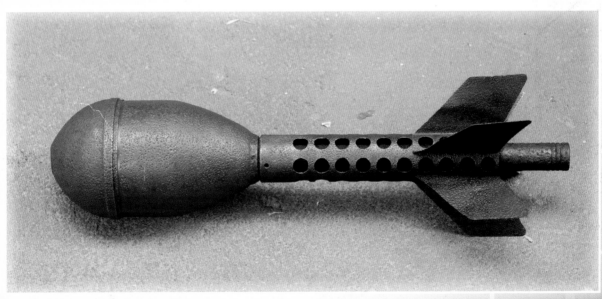

German mortar shell from World War II

INDEX

The Author

Chris Oxlade is an experienced author of educational books for children, with more than 200 titles to his name, including many on science and technology. He enjoys camping and adventurous outdoor sports, including rock climbing, hill running, kayaking and sailing. He lives in England with his wife, children and dogs.

Picture Credits (abbreviations: t = top; b = bottom; c = centre; l = left; r = right)
© www.shutterstock.com:

3 c, 9 c, 11 bl, 13 tr, 14 br, 18 tl, 20 b, 21 tl, 28 tl, 28 bc, 29 tl, 29 bl, 30 br, 31 tc, 31 bc, 32 r.

FC, c = Cody Images. 2, l = 615 Collection/ Alamy Stock Photo. 4, c = Andrew Harker / Alamy Stock Photo. 6, b = Cody Images. 7, c = Cody Images. 8, all = Cody Images. 11, t = Niday Picture Library / Alamy Stock Photo. 12, tl = Cody Images. 12, b = © Boykov / Shutterstock.com. 14, cl = Andrew Bargery / Alamy Stock Photo. 15, t = Cody Images. 15, b = INTERFOTO / Alamy Stock Photo. 16, t = Chronicle / Alamy Stock Photo. 16, b = Military Images / Alamy Stock Photo. 17, b = Cody Images. 19, t = World History Archive / Alamy Stock Photo. 20, tl = Cody Images. 21, b = Cody Images. 22, cl = ITAR-TASS Photo Agency / Alamy Stock Photo. 22, b = Oliver Bunic / Bloomberg / Bloomberg via Getty Images. 22-23, c = PJF Military Collection /Alamy Stock Photo. 23, t = Cody Images. 24, cl = Cody Images. 24-25, c = andrew chittock / Alamy Stock Photo. 25, t = Cody Images. 29, cr = Everett Collection Historical / Alamy Stock Photo.